BLESSINGS
WITHOUT KNOWING
GOD WAS
REALLY THERE

BLESSINGS
WITHOUT KNOWING
GOD WAS
REALLY THERE

VOL. 3

with

OSCAR DIXON, SR

PTP

Pure Thoughts Publishing, LLC

DEDICATION

Rev. Frank D. Dixon Mrs. Ethel M. Dixon

During my youth, I don't remember home life with an uncomfortable lifestyle; our parents had a harmonious relationship. I don't remember loud, boisterous voices and disagreements coming through the house in the midst of seven children.

My innocence betrayed me as I grew older: what I was experiencing was not the norm in other homes; we had hard times, shortages of everything, but the love of our parents for us and the Lords, words can't describe.

My dad and mother were always hugging and playing with us, and I didn't know it then, but there were spiritual blessings of impartation placed in our lives. We grew up passing on to our children what we received from our parents, the Lord of their lives, is the Lord of our lives, and we believe the Lord brought the parents up the rough side of the mountain and set them on a solid foundation in Christ Jesus the Solid Rock, and so it is with us. I dedicate these writings and testimonies to our parents and sisters and brothers; to tell the story is to be in concert with our upbringing.

INTRODUCTION

My Journey; Not Knowing God; Was Really There

THE WRITING OF THIS BOOK IS A SPIRITUAL FOCUS.

I. MY JOURNEY; WITHOUT KNOWING GOD; WAS REALLY THERE

My journey began in my youth, as early as I can remember, with my father and mother, two sisters and four brothers. It continues today, and I have taken stock and realized that the Lord Jesus Christ is my presence help.

II. I SURRENDER ALL:

Things were happening to me and for me. I am trying to take inventory of my life. I knew in my heart that Mother was gone to glory and now Dad as well has been called home. Early one Sunday morning the

Lord gave me this song, "I SURRENDER ALL." I realize going forward perhaps I would be going through spiritual cleansing.

My writing is of the Lord and I must be clear and balanced in my work.

III. FOR, I AM DOING A NEW THING:

When I read this scripture, Isaiah 43:18-19, the presence of the Holy Spirit was so fulfilling. I was in tears, the Lord was speaking. The System Operator at the Rehabilitation Center gave me that scripture to read. The scripture represents The Lord's Exodus out of Egypt was enormous with Moses, but the Lord is saying now, that was minor compared to what is coming.

Chapter One

CAN I TRUST YOU

Ecclesiastes 11:1-2 (NIV) Cast your bread upon the
waters, for after many days you will find it again. (2).
Give a portion to seven, yes even to eight for you do
not know what disaster may come upon the land.

I WAS AT A local church, and the minister was preaching
that he had been led by the Spirit to give away a specific
amount of funds, and when I heard this, I said this is
possible, but there must have been a measure of doubt.
The next morning, I was asleep when the Holy Spirit
put this into my spirit: I saw myself going along the
highway, one that looked something like 285 along
the exit of Jonesboro Road, where I then saw myself
talking to some fellows that were out waiting to be
picked up for a job that morning.

It was amazingly clear that the Holy Spirit had
given me this assignment, and I believe it came about
perhaps because the Holy Spirit recognized the doubt

in my heart the previous night when I was in church and heard the confession of the minister when he was preaching about hearing and obeying the Holy Spirit.

I wasn't certain how to start this effort that I call gifting; I remembered Jonesboro Road from my vision, so I headed over there and circled the service station at least two times, trying to decide who to talk with first. I saw three fellows off to my right, so I parked and went over to speak, but assured them I wasn't picking them up for work. I offered to treat them to something hot to drink, and shortly after that I took out some funds and gave a bit to each of the three fellows, and prayed for them and left. As I went back down Jonesboro Road, I saw a fellow at the exit. I gave him funds as well and went home, but I felt so uncomfortable; I couldn't help wondering, what was this all about?

Later that afternoon, I was truly disturbed about my assignment. Was the Holy Spirit testing me to see if I could be trusted? I decided I better make certain all the funds I was assigned to gift out were met. When I added up the monies that had been gifted already, I realized I had work to do. I went east on 285 West to Hwy 139, then went west and stopped along the road. I saw a young man that said he had three children, so I prayed with him and issued him a gift from the Lord. I went across the street from the hardware store and talked with four men that were sitting around, and I joined them and invited them to have prayer. After prayer, I gave each of them funds, and the one with the walking stick said, "What about me, I am crippled; I should get a couple of extra dollars." The spirit said to me, and I repeated it to him, that being crippled was all in his mind. He looked me in the eyes very strongly, stepping back from the car, and said, "You are right." I believe the Holy Spirit touched him and he became afraid because a stranger shouldn't have known he was not crippled. The Lord had spoken.

As we read these testimonies and the kind of exchanges I had, these were very dangerous areas, and I was very cautious when I spoke to the four men. I didn't leave my car, I prayed with my eyes open, and I didn't turn my car engine off. Once I busted the guy with the walking cane, I knew it was time to leave the block. I departed the area onto Hwy 139 West, and I felt I had to tell someone about this turn of events that had evolved since that early morning. I called cousin Johnson and when she answered, I said, "Hello, this is Oscar." She started crying, and I was saddened by the depth of her sobbing. The Holy Spirit had brought her into my life a few months before. I began to pray for her; I know prayer works, for she had prayed me through some long nights and never-ending days. Through her tears, she kept thanking the Lord, and I wasn't certain why. After I finished my prayer she had calmed down, so I told her my story, which had begun early that morning, and it was now around 05:00 pm and I was en route to a near by church for service.

I told her my story, and she said this was very possible; what became astounding, was her story, because she had been driving up from Alabama to Upstate, Georgia, and was in sincere prayer when the phone rang. When I said, "Oscar," this brought on the tears, because her prayer was telling the Holy Spirit her cell phone was out of minutes and about to be cut off, and she heard in her spirit to call Oscar, to which she said, no way am I going to call him and ask for help—then her phone rang, because I had heard in my spirit to call cousin Johnson.

The Holy Spirit told her the cell phone was her ministry, that is when she heard in her spirit to call Oscar, and she said, "I could never call and ask anyone for funds," and she heard in her spirit, "YOU HAVE NOT, BECAUSE YOU ASK NOT."

After service, I added up the funds I had gifted out earlier, and it was not enough. I was incomplete, on checking my numbers, I still had money to give out. It was after 09:00 p.m., and I wondered where to give out the remainder. On the way home, I saw a service station, as I got closer, I saw a young man sweeping up debris around the outside of the station. I pulled in and spoke to him. I said, "I have something for you." He told me his story, which he had been incarcerated and was trying to work and stay clean. He had three children, and his boss had promised to promote him. I asked him if we could pray, that I would ask the Lord to bless his life. Afterward, I gave him the money and left.

I passed that station the next night and many times since, and I have never seen that young man again. My friend suggested that he was the angel that was sent in my pathway to help me fulfill my assignment because I was committed to obedience to the Lord.

TRANSLATION:

For us, life involves risk and opportunity; there are no guarantees, so we are to be prepared. We shouldn't trust industry, things of man, because he can't guarantee your future. But although life is uncertain, it does not mean we should do nothing. We need a spirit of trust and adventure, facing life's risks and opportunities with God-directed motivation and faith.

Chapter Two

I WAS MOVED

I King 17:24 (NIV) Then the woman said to Elijah, "Now I know that you are a man of God and that the word of the Lord from your mouth is the truth."

I KNOW NOT THE mind of Christ when the minister preaches a powerful message and the Spirit speaks profoundly through this message to me; I believe the Holy Spirit is teaching me to hear and understand. Perhaps this is also a period of growth that the Holy Spirit is taking me through; I believe this part of my teaching for I believe He is my teacher. As I prepared to write this, I felt the Holy Spirit, for the message is received.

The Minister preached a powerful word today, "When The Brook Dries Up": it was time to move for Elijah, who had fled Jezebel and was in the brook Cherith, where the raven fed him daily, and he drank from the brook. The Minister preached that Elijah was safe until the brook went dry. God sends Elijah on his next mission, and the widower and her son would receive God's saving grace.

The word here is to be able to hear the voice of God and be obedient to the word of God. While in church service, I read verse 17:24 and was convicted to tears by the prompting of the Holy Spirit. (24) And the woman said to Elijah, now by this I know that thou art a man of God and that the word of the Lord in thy mouth is truth.

As the Minister continued to preach with power and authority, he said, "God knows what you are going through, and must go through because of where He is taking us." I was filled with the presence of the Holy Spirit and was in tears because of His presence.

The Lord is a wonder, and we don't know the mind of God, so we will trust Him and pray to be obedient to His calling.

TRANSLATION:

Those who have had encounters with men and women, that are called by Jesus the Christ, they will witness that this is the Lord's prophet, whom he has called to do great works. Those who have had prayer, hands laid upon them or a particular anointing, will tell the story that the presence of the Holy Spirit was evident and their situation was made better.

Those who have had these blessings, and those of us that will receive the blessing, I encourage you to receive the blessing in great faith and walk in it, believing that which you have prayed for; you have already received and celebrated to God be the glory.

Chapter Three

SOWING SEEDS FOR HARVEST

Luke 15:1 (NIV) Now the tax collectors and sinners were all gathering around to hear him.

THE LORD BLESSED ME with an excellent message, for I acknowledge that He is the Vine and we are His branches. The brothers Douglas and James were there, starting the service with song, testimonies that prepared us to receive a word from the Holy Ghost. Many times, mothers and fathers came over and brought their children to our corner where the Lord had sent His Word. Many who hear the word mission perhaps get the feeling of missionaries going up and over hills in foreign countries, spreading the good news of God and His ever-present help, waiting with outstretched arms to hold us for we are, His own creation, both Jews, and Gentiles. The Holy Spirit wants us here and now, Evangelizing his children in the parks, highway underpasses, and many other locations; they need to know the Holy Spirit, who was sent to us, is a comforter and counselor for all of us and the lost.

I told them about my mission field; I had been there two years in succession, with medical and evangelism assistance for the many. You'll not see more pain and hunger than as we walked among the many. I opened the doors and invited those who would believe in the name of Jesus Christ our Lord and Savior and were willing to give their life to Him to speak. A young man came forward and confessed he was saved and had given up his old habits. That was an inspiring moment, which we had brought another of the lost sheep to Christ Jesus.

I believe if we continue to bear witness to the word of God, on our mission corners, parks and streets, we will be SOWING SEEDS FOR HARVEST. I tell the listeners that I am a farmer's son, I grew up plowing and toiling the land for preparation to sow the seeds, and we would maintain that crop through due season expecting a good yield. Farmers are taught to sow with expectancy. So is His word that has been sowed since the beginning of time, so those who would believe are saved and are called children of God.

TRANSLATION:

Jesus came to set the captives free. Jesus risked defilement by touching those who had leprosy and by neglecting to wash in the prescribed manner. In Jesus, there was no certain class of people he kept with; he went where he was needed, to offer salvation to all sinners. Jesus did not worry about his reputation being founded among the poor and needy.

Chapter Four

ROUGH ROAD AHEAD

I Kings 19:5 (NIV) Then he lay down under the tree and fell asleep. All at once an angel touched him and said, "Get up and eat."

OUR MINISTER ON THIS Sunday was feeding the flock at the Lord's house. He was in the Word, from the title, "More Bark Than Bite," a very powerful message concerning the work and efforts of the Apostle of the Lord. After Elijah had done a powerful work assigned him by the Holy Spirit, he perhaps felt tired and couldn't be as engaging in the service for the Lord; in today's society, we call this work burn-out and know we need to take a set time of rest and recovery. In most cases the Lord warns us to take rest so we can get back to the assignment the Lord has already planned for us.

Our Faith is in the Lord, and we have assignments; the Holy Spirit will not leave us in these troubled times, for the Holy Spirit has promised to always be with us, and never to leave us. Elijah was running from Jezebel, who was angry for losing her four hundred prophets, slain by the sword. Jezebel promised the same would happen to Elijah, so he ran for his life, tired, weak, and alone. He fell asleep under a juniper tree and was awakened by the angels of God, with water and food that they had prepared for him.

The minister preached that when we come off fast, we are prepared for a long, hard journey. God is getting ready to take us someplace, and we will need all our strength, energy and faith for the journey. This part of his message was overpowering, and the presence of the Holy Spirit was so fulfilling I couldn't hold back the tears. This compelling word tells me that I am headed into "Rough Road Ahead," and the Holy Spirit is preparing me. I have already encountered storms in my life that seemed endless.

I received this scripture more than once. I was in church when the minister was preaching, and I felt the presence of the Holy Spirit when the minister read the scripture. On another occasion, I was at home and went to my kitchen to get something, and laying on the floor, a sticker had fallen from the refrigerator door; I picked it up and read it and felt the presence of the Holy Spirit very strongly. I wondered, what did it mean? The scripture: I believe drawing closer to the Lord Jesus in all things is a journey that perhaps is the road that I must stay on, establishing a closer relationship with Jesus Christ. I encouraged everyone that's going into issues, personal or otherwise, make certain you take the Lord in the battle with you. My testimony says He is our risen savior and in I Peter 2:24: Who his own self-bare our sins in his own body on the tree, that we, being dead to sins, should live unto righteousness: By whose stripes ye are healed. He is the Lord of miracles, signs, and wonders.

TRANSLATION:

God First let Elijah rest and eat, after leading him out of depression from job burn-out. Then God confronted him with the need to return to his mission, to speak God's words in Israel. Elijah's battles were not over; he still had work to do. When you feel let down after a great spiritual experience, remember that God's purpose for your life is not yet over.

Chapter Five

GOD ANSWER'S PRAYER

Psalm 91:15 (NIV) He will call upon me, and I will answer him, I will be with him in trouble, I will deliver him and honor him.

SISTER FRANKIE HAD PRAYED a prayer that only her and the Master had shared, and I was a party to the desire of her heart. I had prayed a desire of my heart on her behalf, asking the Holy Spirit to bless my prayer because I thought it was so important; I placed it before the Holy Spirit for his guidance and answers.

Sister Frankie had been battling knee problems for many years, after working in nursing care her full life until forced retirement. The pain finally drew a decision to have knee replacement surgery, and with that decision, she prayed that she wanted me to be there. I traveled from Georgia to New York for her surgery, accompanied by my wife, and met my sister, Reverend Nancy, and brother James and my former pastor was there.

I thank God for traveling mercies; we was able to be there with her and talk with the doctor, and my former pastor had prayer early that morning. When sister Frankie went off to surgery, we sat in the waiting room, it seemed an eternity. While waiting, Rev. Nancy invited me to go up and visit a family friend's daughter, who had serious, critical surgery and had not responded well.

When I came over to her, she seemed to remember me from when I lived in Westchester. While there, I was prompted to pray for her. Rev. Nancy and I prayed mightily on her behalf, and I was careful to give my God all the praise and all the glory, for He is worthy. After I finished praying a few minutes later, she sat up in bed, I believe she began eating food. We were overjoyed at the work of the Lord. A few weeks later, I received a call that this young lady was completely healed and went home.

Sister Frankie came out of surgery in excellent and rare form; it seemed the Lord had taken up her pain, and I received a prompting from the Holy Spirit that she should not be complaining or murmuring, for He had answered her prayer. She said to me, at a later date, the Lord told her He had answered her prayer and brought me there with his blessing powers so that God would be glorified and others would believe.

Remembering through our testimonies, God's promises are true; others will take hold of the testimonies and become believers and become new sons and daughters in the family of Our Lord and Savior Jesus Christ. We are Kingdom builders for the Kingdom of God.

TRANSLATION:

It is comforting to know that God watches over us even in times of great stress and fear. When we are asking God for deliverance and healing, we must understand it can only come to pass if it's in His Will.

Chapter Six

A DREAM COMES TRUE I: SOUTH AFRICA

Colossians 1:27 (NIV) To them God chosen to make known among the Gentiles the glorious riches of this mystery, which is Christ in you, the hope of glory.

WHEN I WAS VERY young, I spent time daydreaming from seeing pictures in my geography books and magazines. My daydreams took their longest journeys when I was working in the hot fields on the farm with my folks as sharecroppers.

When I was in high school, we were sharecropping on this property, and I became the son that was assigned to help tend his milk cow and horses. This effort generated a job working on the Institute for them and a payday for my help. Our youth would laugh heartedly today at the idea of working all day for twenty or thirty cents a day and then walking one-and-a-half hours to get from the Institute to the farm. What was painful about the walk home was that my neighbors would pass me, walking briskly, trying to reach home before dark and avoid becoming a target for Caucasians in possible attacks while walking.

When working at the customer's house, I would find books thrown away and along the roadside walking home with books to read such as Reader's Digest, and books on geography of other countries. This heightened my desire to travel to Africa, I coined a phrase that said, "I desire to walk in the waters of my ancestors." God does look at the heart because he knew what was in my dreaming was founded in the deep recesses of my being.

When we saw Tarzan in the jungle with Jane, they were entangled with the natives, with spears chasing them; we never got to see clearly in the villages, where starvation, sickness, and disease were evident. Never the less, my dreams were etched in my heart to go and see for myself and, perhaps, do something that would help my sisters and brothers.

I thought if I got to South Africa, Johannesburg, I hoped to visit President Mandela's home and perhaps get a glimpse of him, his churches, and the places where they held their secret meetings during the reign of terror by Apartheid.

When I was very young, daydreaming daily, I never thought that I would fail to get there. These are big dreams for a little boy down in Alabama, where we lived as sharecroppers and my dad, the Rev. Frank D. Dixon, was an A.M.E. Zion Pastor, where there was practically no income. You would find me many days in the barn reading the founded Reader's Digest and others books or magazines that increased my imagination.

I did get that long-awaited blessing to go to Johannesburg, South Africa, and other countries. When the Lord God Almighty says He looks at the heart, it is gospel truth. The Lord knew my heart's desire and brought it to fruition.

Finally, one afternoon I received a call from my son, Oscar Lee, inviting me to a dinner prepared by his neighbor. When I arrived at dinner that evening, prepared by his friend for my daughter-in-law, in late November 2000, my son encouraged me to talk about his planned trip to Johannesburg and on to Cape Town, South Africa. In January 2001, my friend enlightened me that he was bringing twenty-five-plus students to South Africa to put in practice modules that would aid businesses in updating to a modern method of operating in Durbin, Johannesburg and Cape Town, South Africa.

This extraordinary man, invited Gloria and I on this trip, separate from his students on their business and learning venture, coupled with time for touring, shopping and other projects.

Just to remind you, The World Trade Center Towers had just been destroyed on September 11, 2000. Gloria and I were in Athens, Greece when the bombing took place, and we were on lockdown over there because the hotel we were in was the secured site for the embassy, so all were moved from the embassy to our hotel, and all communication was cut off until they could investigate how widespread this terrorist attack existed.

We couldn't communicate by telephones, computer, or e-mail to reach family back home. About three nights later, we received a call on my purchased cell phone that all was well. We let go a big sigh of relief because we have sisters and brothers and other family and friends in New York. Gloria quickly reminded me we had been stranded in Athens, Greece. Our tour took us into Turkey, and it was rather frightening with the air base in Turkey; the United States are based there, we had supersonic jets giving the cruise ship partial escort through their waters.

I knew the Lord had smile on me and blessed this trip for me because no one could have written a more perfect script on how this scene played out. Undoubtedly this was a move of the Lord, and I am thankful today and feel so blessed to have traveled to these countries, and was anticipating even then to return with Gloria. I thought I would tell her about the huge shopping malls outside of Johannesburg and Cape Town that is walking distance from the hotels.

My heart leaped with joy when that Delta Airline #747 set down at the Johannesburg International Airport; we had reached the motherland and were looking forward to"Walking in The Waters of our Ancestors". We visited the island of Sanitorini, Patmos where Disciple John wrote Revelation.

This shall be recorded on The Staff where a move of the Lord had placed me into this most excellent position.

TRANSLATION:

Paul, the disciple, declares that God's plan is a "mystery that has been kept hidden for ages and generations," not in the sense it was hidden for a few to know about, but it was hidden until Christ came. Through Christ, it was made open to all. God's secret plan is "Christ in you, the hope of glory." God planned to have his Son, Jesus Christ, live in the heart of all who believe in Him, even Gentiles like the Colossians.

Christ isn't hidden if you will come to Him. We pray in our hearts, dreams that we have, and our Lord looks at our hearts, and there He decides to fulfill our dreams. He can do all things if we trust Him.

Chapter Seven

THE GREATER GLORY

I Corinthian 2:9 (NIV) No eye has seen, no ear has heard, no mind has conceived what God has prepared for those who love him.

THOSE OF US WHO are Christian realize that Our God has a purpose for our lives from the beginning. Many of us who are in that arena with one foot in the world and one foot with good intention but it's not on solid ground, we have lessons to learn. We need to be certain that we are all the way in and are strengthening our position every day in The Lord. I struggle everyday trying to get it right, I heard in my spirit early one morning, Oscar, "get closer to the cross," you guess correctly, hearing that frighten me, this was over two years ago this 2018. I am trying to be diligent in drawing nearer to the Lord, it is good to be trusted with His Word and children. I felt His presence when I typed those last two lines.

When we give our life to Christ Jesus, we have submitted to following after Him and giving up doing it our way. It isn't easy, but God will tell you, like He has told others, trust me for I am meek and kind, my yoke is light, for I will never leave you, nor forsake you.

I write this now because I was convicted by this when I read the scripture on how Jacob held onto the angel and daybreak was upon him, but Jacob refused to let go until The Angel of the Lord blessed him. Many of us have that desire. I encourage each of us not to quit because we are "Jacob Seekers" and we won't let go until you bless us. There is that generation waiting on Jacob's Promise.

The Lord said to me, if I don't take you through this now, you won't be able to handle the greater things I have in store for you. This is the chastening rod of God to train us in the way He would have us go, and as we receive greater responsibility, we won't stray from his teaching. When the Holy Spirit has brought us into right standing with Him, whereas He can trust us with His name, His Word, with power and authority to declare things as if they already were. You will realize we have greater authority to use the name of Jesus.

The Holy Spirit promises us that The Greater Glory is coming and is about to fall on us; when I heard this, I felt convicted by The Holy Spirit. When the blessings of our Lord Jesus Christ start to flow, know that you will draw the enemy and in these encounters, always praise God first, no matter how bad it gets; don't faint, but go to your knees and thank God for being in our encounters with us, because He promised to never to leave us, nor forsake us, that He will be with us always.

The prompting on The Holy Spirit tells me those that I bless in His name will be made whole in His name by their faith.

TRANSLATION:

We cannot imagine all that God has in store for us, both in this life and for eternity. He will create a new heaven and a new earth, and we will live with Him forever. Until then, His Holy Spirit comforts and guides us. God has a wonderful eternal future for us, so have hope and courage to press on in this life, to endure hardship and to avoid giving in to temptation.

Chapter Eight

HE PROMISED TO BLESSED "HIM" II

Samuel II 7:28 (NIV) And now, O Lord God, thou art that God, and thy words be true, and thou hast promised this goodness unto thy servant:

IN JANUARY 2008, I was down at my barn on a Monday morning. My truck radio was on, and I heard this announcement, a young Senator from Chicago had thrown his hat into the ring for the Presidential office of the United States. The name I didn't recognize, but I realized he was an Afro-American and I said to myself out loud, "Lord can this man win?" I heard in my spirit, "If he runs, he'll win." I felt the Holy Spirit very strongly, and I believed then what I had heard in my spirit, from the Holy Spirit.

Two years later, February 25, 2009, the Holy Spirit delivered on His word when President Barack Obama stood before Congress and laid out a sweeping vision of an America transformed. It was everything that millions of us across the country voted for: he spoke of an America that leads the world in clean energy innovation, a country in which every citizen can see a doctor when there is a need.

A nation with a thriving economy that benefits all of us, not just those at the top. The most crucial thing he said that night? "Suffer no illusions that this will be an easy process; it'll be hard."

When I read this from President Barack Obama, tears came to my eyes from the presence of the Holy Spirit that filled me, and I heard in my spirit that the Lord would bless His servant to have a successful administration. I thank the Lord for insight and revelation from the beginning that Barack Obama would win his presidential election and have a successful campaign in his presidential office.

Racism has shown its true colors since this election, with even talk show hosts having vehemently declared to do everything in their power to make certain this President failed. If that was not enough, The Supreme Court of The United States of America opened the floodgates to permit large companies to supply unlimited monies to campaigns, practically guaranteeing the ability to buy the desires of their hearts. If the Lord brought you into this work, He is bound by His word to bring you through it. I believe God has a provision for the vision He gives us. This election has historical value, for those who thought this was a lucky outpouring, the

Lord said not so, the things He ordained is done, to make certain the people know that the Lord has done this. President Barack Obama wins a second term, and in this historical win, he won with the Electoral College and The Popular Vote handily. I will record this historical event on "The Moses Staff."

TRANSLATION:

A follower of Jesus Christ becomes sanctified, set apart for sacred use, cleansed, and made holy through believing and obeying the Word of God. Daily application of God's Word has a purifying effect on our minds and hearts.

Chapter Nine

"CONFESSION" JOINT HEIRS WITH CHRIST

> Romans 8:17 Now if we are children, then we are heirs; heirs of God and joint-heirs with Christ, if indeed we share in his sufferings so that we may also share in his glory.

I HAVEN'T BEEN ABLE to connect this word and scripture, but if not now, perhaps at a later time. I received this early one morning, between 03:30 and 05:00, and I wrote it down. This word came towards me like a book front that said "confession" and the cover front of the book looked purple or lavender. When it was upon me, it said "Confession," and following after that very early morning, I received scripture, Romans 8:17, and I felt The Holy Spirit, and I was disturbed, frightened if you will, when I remembered the way the word "confession" came forward to me like a book cover and the scripture came a few minutes later, and a song came, "I must tell Jesus." The song left me humming continually. I have heard it preached that when the Lord gives you a song to sing, it's to keep you until He answers your prayer. When I wrote this down, the presence of the Holy Spirit was so strong, that He brought tears to my eyes. I began to study to see what all this meant, so I studied these particular words and statement.

Confession was the word the spirit gave me, and I received the scripture Romans 8:17, and it said: And if children, then heirs: heirs of God, and joint heirs with Christ: if so be that we suffer with Him, that we may also be glorified together.

Joint Heirs, we witness each day Gentiles and Israelites are joint heirs, sharing in the blessing of God. It's one who obtains something assigned to himself with sharing with others a joint participation.

Heirs is a messianic usage, one who receives his allotted possession by right of sonship: So of Christ as all things being subject to His way of Christians as exalted by faith to the dignity of sons of Abrahams and sons of God, and hence to receive the blessing of God's Kingdom promised to Abraham.

Purple is a distinguishing color used as the robe on Jesus Christ to mock Him, this purple Robe is And Emblem of Royalty.

TRANSLATION:

Likewise, when a person becomes a Christian, he or she gains all the privileges and responsibilities of a child in God's family. One of these outstanding privileges is being led by the Holy Spirit.

Because we are already given His best gifts: His Son, His Holy Spirit, forgiveness, and eternal life; and He encourages us to ask Him for whatever we need.

Chapter Ten

THE HOLY SPIRIT SPEAKS

Isaiah 57:18 I have seen his ways, but I will heal him;
I will guide him and restore comfort to him.

ON A FRIDAY NIGHT, Saturday morning, after 03:00 am, I got this heavy dream in which the Holy Spirit spoke and told me I have a problem with my colon and I woke in a fearful sweat. I went to my restroom and returned to bed, but sleep was far from me. I got up and went to my prayer room, had scripture and prayer, and lay on my couch in meditation. After a while in meditation, there came this quiet but very clear voice, and it told me to eat small amounts and stay hungry while I get well. Truly, the Holy Spirit speaks, and I am so blessed that the blessing of the Lord spoke to me.

This issue began in March 2010 into 2011, and it has taken all the prayers of myself and others to help me keep hope alive, for the Holy Spirit is still working this to a complete healing. This testimony is going forth, thanking the Holy Spirit for keeping me, for His patience and great love for me. Through all the days I didn't feel so well, many days I raised up and went out, visited nursing and care facilities. It is amazing, the presence of the Holy Spirit working through me, the blessing of healing, converts to Christ Jesus fresh anointing, blessing people's homes and their businesses.

Surely the Lord is worthy to be praised and worshipped. I couldn't have kept myself going; it was the Holy Spirit working through me that kept me spiritually charged, to help others, and took my cares and put them after the cares of others. Time and time again, when I was least expecting of anything, someone would call or send a much needed scripture and prayer that changed my demeanor and gave me reasons to keep the faith and continue to do the work of the Lord.

Those conversations and dreams in the night were frightening, but never the less, very encouraging.

We must remember, if we are trying to be faithful to our calling, surely the Holy Spirit speaks to us, and He is our ever-present help in everything. Our daily walk in good health, or if you and the families are having the best of times or the worst of times, He is with us.

TRANSLATION:

Those of us who are humble and repentant, the high and Holy God came down to our level to save us because, it is impossible for us to go up to His level to save ourselves

Chapter Eleven

BARBERSHOP PRAYERS

Matthew 18:19; Again, I tell you that if two of you on earth agree about anything you ask for, it will be done for you by my Father in heaven.

I HAD AN APPOINTMENT for a haircut on Saturday morning at 09:30 at the barbershop. She was late I went next door and talked with the fuel desk attendant. She said I know, your son. He brings his buses to the truck stop and fuel them. She admired his respect and kindness toward others. She saw him fueling the buses so his female drivers wouldn't need to, and she thought that was so admirable. We don't often see gentleman like him.

I thought I felt the Holy Spirit, I asked her if she had been praying about something, she hadn't but her friend was dealing with issues. At the presence of the Holy Spirit, I offer her information concerning a very good health clinic that can help her friend.

I was finally in the barber chair getting my hair cut, and a couple of gentlemen came in for their hair cuts, and a few minutes later, one adult and three children. What caught my eye was that the third child was being carried by what looked to be a 15-or 16-year-old. The little guy was curled up in his arm and looked to be about 50 pounds and very fragile, with small arms and legs.

A few minutes later, I felt The Holy Spirit, and when I said I was not going to bother with that situation, I got a fulfilling nudging. So I said under my breath that I would pray within for him, saying nothing out loud. I began to pray within myself and that fulfilling nudge came back so strongly, I couldn't help but cry, and the voice in my spirit said, "Pray for him, I will bless him." I heard this and felt this in my spirit so strongly that I stopped the barber and told her I needed two minutes of her time because the Holy Spirit was all over me, and I was in tears, I then called the young teenager and said, "Bring me the baby over," I asked the adult male if I could pray for his child, he said go ahead.

The Holy Spirit was so powerful and presence that I felt there was a healing would take place: When I had finished, I reminded them to receive the healing as if it had already been done. After a few minutes passed, I heard this food that the child would need to get stronger to carry his fragile body, and I gave this to the Uncle to write down. As the barber was finishing up, I told them to put the child down and let him walk, and he did this quickly, and the little guy took a couple of steps with them holding his arms, and I confess that I was so thankful that The Lord had touched this Child's life. The barber was shampooing my hair so my head was all the way back and I couldn't see. When I sat up, the little child, with his helper, had walked across the floor and I marveled at the work of the Holy Spirit.

There was a caucausian, middle-aged man sitting, waiting for his hair cut, but had been curious as to what was happening with me and the child. The Holy Spirit wasn't finished; I felt His presence in my spirit tell me let the man know he is called out for ministry and to give his life to Christ Jesus, he didn't seem surprise, and didn't reply. This I did, and explained to him the approach, and these things would come to pass. I also blessed the two young men, but Uncle had left.

For me, this was such a powerful intervention by the Holy Spirit for that family and my barber. I reminded her that months ago, I prayed, blessed her shop, and the Lord promised to bless her shop, so she had to get herself in place to receive the extra customers. I told her at the front desk she had missed two customers already, and I had been waiting since 09:30 am that Saturday morning, with six people waiting to get their hair cut. I am so humble to have this experience, through the Holy Spirit.

TRANSLATION:

Jesus looked ahead to a new day when He would be present with His followers not in the body, but through His Holy Spirit. In the body of believers (the church), the sincere agreement of two people is more powerful than the superficial agreement of thousands, because Christ's Holy Spirit is with them. Two or more believers "filled with the Holy Spirit," will pray according to God's will, not their own, thus their requests will be granted.

Chapter Twelve

GOD'S WORK IN PROGRESS

Proverb 17:9 (NIV) He who covers over an offensive promotes love, but whoever repeats the matter separates close friends.

I AM CONTINUALLY IN prayer for our youth they are under the watchful eye of the Holy Spirit. I acknowledge that we are warring against the enemy and our youth and ourselves are under constant attack. When we encounter our youth with rudeness, disobedience, we need to be aware and be prepared to help support and bring understanding. If we observe carefully, we will get the opportunity.

On this Sunday in church, a young man of perhaps 14 years old was texting, and his mother and sister tried to get him to stop, and he refused to give up the phone or stop texting while the minister was in the midst of his sermon. The young man was sitting next to my wife on the right side, so I reached over her and touched him and looked him in the eyes, and he handed his mother the phone. A few minutes later, he was in front of my wife going for communion, and I touched his shoulder and said, "My name is Oscar, would you pull your pants up some?" and he said yes. His demeanor had changed completely since our first encounter, where he was friendly toward his family. My prayer partner said when I touched him, he felt the Holy Spirit and was given a good attitude. I know for myself, while the minister was closing in his message, he said that if we work toward the glory of God, that everything we touch or place our feet upon, the Lord would bless; I felt the Holy Spirit and felt blessed.

I have had several conversations with my young friend that work for me, encouraging him to believe that the Lord wants him to do well. I asked my friend if he remembered what the Holy Spirit prompted me to tell him. The Holy Spirit said that He would save my friend in spite of himself. I asked him to apply for his certificate to become a chauffeur; this is an on-road for a better salary and would help provide for a better lifestyle and other necessities of life. I reminded him that he has improved his lifestyle and work ethic, but that there are things he needs to remove from his life to show a better, improved spiritual walk.

I asked him to pray with me about what he wanted to give up towards developing a better spiritual lifestyle. I reminded him that The Lord has blessed us enormously, and asked him what he would be willing to change. My friend prayed a very powerful and sound prayer on giving up some issues that have troubled his life, and he desired to turn them over to The Lord. For me, this is the beginning of a turn-around that we need to see in so many of our youth today.

TRANSLATION:

This proverb is saying that we should be willing to forgive others' sins against us. Try never to bring anything into an argument that is unrelated to the topic being discussed. As we grow to be more like Christ, we will acquire God's ability to forget the confessed sins of the past.

Chapter Thirteen

HIS MESSAGE IS CLEAR

HAGGAI 1:13 Then spake Haggai the Lord's messenger in the Lord's message unto the people, saying, I am with you, saith The Lord.

I WENT TO OUR community church today, to hear our minister teach and preach, it brought back memories of old. He preached on a very interesting topic, The School of The Prophets being transparent.

Shortly after we had lunch, I was sitting with a few friends talking about days gone past that we often refer to as the good old days. If any of us have a desire to get involved in visiting rehab centers, feed the hungry, our school need our assistance, our children need our support, you would be surprise how many children would love a hug today. If we have a desire to see change, "the Lords says he is with us." Our opportunity is now.

A church friend came and sat with us, next to me, and I spoke to her. I had not seen her that often because she was supporting other places.

I felt the prompting of the Holy Spirit to pray for her, with blessings to come, and there would be something happening soon, I suggested to her. When I had finished praying, she told me she had received the prayer, then she looked at me and said, "There is something different about you." I felt quite full already from the moving of the spirit in our prayer. I felt a continued urging to Anoint her with Authority to speak in Jesus's name, for me, she has been called into the ministry to serve the one true, living God. To those that hear her will feel that it was specifically for them through the Authority of God and his word would be upon them. Family this is power from on high given unto men to fulfill the purpose the Lord has plan for our life in Him.

Jesus's message is clear: He is raising up prepared worshippers, that will forge the war with the enemy to take back the church and prepare for the return of Our Savior. We must spread the glory of God in every stronghold and nation that we have the opportunity to tread in with great authority.

TRANSLATION:

When the Lord sent his messenger, there had to be a reminder to the people that the Lord is in everything; their crops of wine of the grapes, grains, and olives were their resources that they depended on. Their farms became their security; meanwhile, they neglected the worship of the Lord, and as a result, he sent a drought to destroy their livelihood and call them back to himself.

The Lord wanted them to know his house of worship was in need of repair and would called his servants into this work.

Chapter Fourteen

GOD IS STILL CALLING US

Thessalonians 3:3 (NIV) But the Lord is faithful, and he will strengthen and protect you from the evil one.

I MET JANICE A few year ago, and immediately I knew she was a woman of God, and she knows he is our savior. A quite soft-spoken woman of God and she speaks of knowing who God is and what he has done for her. For a young woman, she demonstrated great faith, it took believing in the Lord that she could raise her young family.

Through our conversations, I realized she had graduated from the school of theology and is very knowledgeable. I remember saying to her, "The Lord has called you to minister, start acting on your call to do works at assisted living homes, hospitals, visiting elderly in our community, and church." I have invited her on occasions to come and visit with me at the community center nursing home to get the feel and learn approaches and see and experience those that need to hear a word from the Holy Spirit while in their situation. She has fulfill this work area and continuing work with young people who need direction and support. I see my young friend work with a purpose, and I witness she has their trust, they are reaching out and receive guidance.

In these areas, the Holy Spirit has a purpose for our calling, to go and preach, pray and teach His word to His children, and He would bless them that call upon His name. She called me today with a testimony that she had and encountered a mother that has a problem with her daughter. She remembered her promise to the Holy Spirit, that she would help others if He brings her through her situations with her children. Today, she remembered that she promised to help others in their storms, and she ministered with the mother and gave her wisdom and understanding that only the Holy Spirit could give her. When I heard this from her and wrote this, I felt the Holy Spirit.

When our friend went to work, so did the spirits; they attacked her. I have said it and heard it preached that when we begin to serve God in our purpose that he has for us, we bring out the evil spirit and it will attack us. If this frightens us, we go back to doing nothing.

We thank the Lord for teaching us how to help others; through Him, we can do powerful works, and acknowledge that aside from Him we can do nothing. Now we praise the Lord and give Him all the glory and honor that is due to His mighty name.

TRANSLATION:

Beneath the surface of our daily routine, a fierce struggle among invisible spiritual powers is being waged. Our sure defense is prayer that God will protect us from the evil one and strengthen us. We will remember to put on the whole armour of God and depend on him to shield us. 1.) Spiritual attacks are real. 2.) Pray for strength and help from God. 3.) Study the Bible and learn Satan's tactics. 4.) Memorize scriptures to support you. 5.) Follow leaders who teach truths to live by. 6.) Practice what you are taught by the sound leaders.

Chapter Fifteen

NEVER ENOUGH PRAISE

Psalm 90:17 (NIV) May the favor of the Lord our
God rest upon us; establish the works of our hands
for us yes, establish the works of our hands.

WHILE I AM IN my studies or writings, occasionally I
hear a quiet voice that elevates me in the time of need;
just when my issues have me continually in prayer, the
Holy Ghost gives me hope. Over three weeks ago, I
heard, "I am healing you," and I heard, "Worship Me."
A week later I heard, "Praise Him." I won't let this
go; it gave me encouragement that I can't explain, it
raised my confidence and strengthened my goings,
and allowed me to continue to do my assignment at
the nursing homes and serve at the Health Center,
along with our Mission Corner, downtown. I urge
anyone who has time, make it a priority to visit nursing
homes and rehabilitation centers and encourage the
families there, that they, aren't forgotten. While I am

there, I bring my Bible and invite the Lord to help me encourage them through prayers, scriptures, and conversation. When I come through the doors, I feel and see the anticipation on their faces. Many of the residents have not seen a family member or visitor in long periods of time, you can see the vital signs leaving them. Whosoever reads this, I hope you are touched by the Holy Spirit of the Lord and become a friend of the friendless; you are welcome to come and be moved to support the residents.

A few days after hearing the encouraging words of healing, I woke up with this song in my mouth and was humming it in bed and out and about. I thank the Holy Spirit for this song, "I look high and low, can't find nobody like You." This is amazing, and I am singing it the best I can, and it feels good. The Holy Spirit is keeping me encouraged while I go through my challenges, and I am not alone. I am so thankful that Christ Jesus is leading and guiding me.

He set me before a powerful natural-pathic doctor, who began my session with prayers of healing, and he generally prays the night before for spiritual guidance, and I pray for the Holy Spirit to bless him with insight for the best results on my visit. His prayers had a powerful anointing on me today, where there were traveling and mission work, both near and abroad, where there is a great need, and I would be well received. My studies and writings will be of great benefit in my works. Beyond the studies and writing the spiritual anointing, he calls me to another level of authority. Their is a call that will go forth, bringing changes and the receiving of the Word of the Lord, bringing the lost to the Lord. This mission work will help establish the building of the Kingdom of God, to whom all the glory belongs. Our Lord promise to return but don't want to return and find us making excuses.

TRANSLATION:

Thankful people can worship wholeheartedly, and gratitude opens our hearts to God's peace and enables us to put on love; discontented people are never satisfied with their lives. To increase our thankfulness, take an inventory of our total possession, and find gratitude and thanks to God, who keeps us. Let's celebrate God's goodness to us, and ask in prayer for all you need in the future.

Chapter Sixteen

HEARING HIS VOICE

I Peter 4-10 (NIV) Each one should use whatever gift he has received to serve others, faithfully administering God's grace in its various forms.

TODAY, I WENT TO the post office to mail a letter, and while on line, I went to the next available post office teller to mail my letters. I greeted the young man and asked him if he had read the scripture that he is named after, and he said, "Yes sir, I have." My next comment was, "your mother is a minister in your house?" He said yes it's my mother, I said, "How would I know?" he said, "The Lord told you." He said from what he received that morning, He saw in his dream, he expected something like this to happen, meaning, in some way, somehow he would receive information and direction about his spiritual journey. There were people waiting their turn in line while I was pressing forward to blessing his life with a call to a ministry in the name of Jesus Christ.

Daniel was one of the earliest prophets of Judah, his frequent calls to blow a trumpet in Zion, to consecrate a fast, to proclaim a solemn assembly, and to gather the people together to come before the Lord. JOEL 2:15

I felt very comfortable when I spoke these words to him, with his pleasantness, kind smile and meek presence, I said to my new friend, "There is a calling on your life to serve the Lord." The Lord was very presence, so I commented, "This isn't the first time you have heard this, but today, you hear clearly, and I would like to pray and anoint blessing over your life." My new friend said thank you that surprised me, and handed me a note with his name and telephone number on it. This young man has something in his gut that want let him have peace, he is a seeker of the Lord who will provide. If you seek me you will find me.

I called my friend to complete our encounter, he is from The Mother Land, and his mother is a minister. He had been in prayer that morning, seeking the presence of the Holy Spirit for understanding, on what he should be doing. He told me he's shy and doesn't speak out because of his shyness. I prayed blessing and anointed him as a servant of the Lord Jesus Christ, called into ministry to do work that has already been purposed for your life from the beginning. You must submit to the Lord and be led by the Holy Spirit, I explained to him with the blessing comes authority to use the name of our Lord Jesus Christ. Through the knowledge of the scriptures, and sitting under his mother's teaching, you will speak with authority, and the power of the Holy Ghost will be upon him, and he'll begin speaking boldly and with authority.

I confessed to him that there will be times he'll need to reach out to someone and he is welcome to call me anytime, day or night. He was very thankful; he then prayed the favor of God over my life, and I felt the prompting of the Holy Spirit, and I thanked him for the blessing.

TRANSLATION:

Our abilities should be faithfully used to serve others; none are for our own exclusive enjoyment. Some use their gifts selfishly, and others are not certain of their abilities; Peter addresses, we are to find our gifts and use them.

Chapter Seventeen

HIS BLESSING FLOWS

1 SAMUEL 6:13 (NIV) Now the people of Beth-Shemesh were harvesting their wheat in the valley, and when they looked up and saw the ark, they rejoiced at the sight.

THE MINISTER WAS PREACHING this powerful sermon from I Samuel: 1-13, and he told the story of a young lady who identified her attacker, and he went to jail. After 11 years, he was set free because DNA testing had come into practice. Ironically, he met the victim and offered her forgiveness for her mistake that cost him 11 years of his life.

We are to be reminded of how we walk, for we have been given a Sacred Assignment; we are future kings. I was affected by verse 13, and when I read this, I felt the prompting of the Holy Spirit. I am not certain what the meaning is; often the message will come to pass soon or be established at a later date.

I Samuel 6:13 And they of Beth-Shemesh in the valley: and they lifted up their eyes, and saw the ark, and rejoiced to see it. In our scripture, it teaches us that wherever the Ark of The Lord goes, a blessing of The Lord follows, so the workers rejoiced and were celebrating for a future blessing that would flow into Israel. For the Philistines, the hand of God was against them, and they sent The Ark into Israel with two cows pulling it, that just had new calves hardly weaned, and the powerful message says milk cows will not leave their newly born, they set them in the right direction without any one guiding. Ordinarily, cows that have new calves would never leave their new suckling calves to pull a cart without a guide to usher them in the right direction, but the Lord wanted the Philistines to see His power and that His hand was against them.

TRANSLATION:

Two cows were taken from their newborn calves unweaned and were yoked together and hooked to the Ark of the Covenant and sent up to Beth-Shemesh. The irony of this is that cows never leave their unweaned calves and take a direction without any ushering of any kind. Only God has power over the natural order and can cause this to happen. God sent the cows to Israel to cancel the attempt by the Philistines and show his mighty power.

Chapter Eighteen

THE MISSION CORNER, SAY YES

Psalm 91:14 (NIV) "Because he loves me," says the Lord, "I will rescue him; I will protect him, for he acknowledges my name."

I MET A FRIEND over five years ago through an elderly furniture repairman. I was moving into our new residence, and while in transition, my 50th birthday present fell off the truck and was damaged badly. My wife or I, saw an ad and called for a repairman and shortly after that, I met, his trainee who eventually came and worked for me in his spare time. On one such occasion, he explained that he worked with the homeless and disadvantaged with the repairman and his wife. They were there for him during a low period in his life.

He was working with me one day, and asked if I would come and speak to the families that he works with and supports in the streets of Atlanta. He believed I could help them, the things I have spoken to him he was moved by the spoken words. I was hesitant, but I promised to make myself available. Down deep, I wasn't totally sincere, but I believe God was listening and guiding me, though I didn't recognize the signs.

There were other times he invited me to join them and speak, I squirmed a noncommittal yes, but without real intent. At this time I had never done street ministry, the invite didn't encourage me.

I didn't see him for months, during that time, the Holy Spirit had begun to shape me. My prayer life was consistent, fasting and bible study, it was good to spend more time with the Lord. I was browsing through my address logger and came upon my new friends cell number. I felt an apology would be the honest thing to do, I called and apologized and said I would keep my word this time, give me a time and place I will meet you and do my best, sincerely you can count on me. I look back on those times and I know that the Holy Spirit led me to look for his phone number in my book by the events that have transpired since then; my steps had to be altered by the Holy Spirit to get me on those corners and care facilities.

That call was over fourteen years ago, and even today, I continue to appear and speak. I have termed the location Our Mission Corner. I prepare sermons that are spirit led and prepared for our Mission Corner, there were three Godly men that are dedicated workers for the Lord. They come each Sunday with hot food, with a full course dinner prepared between 09:45 am until finish at about 11:30, and service is held between those hours. The message through The Holy Spirit has been so fulfilling, the lost have come to Christ Jesus on that corner. I confess it was very kind and hospitable, of them, I certainly didn't deserve it, but they gave me the opportunity each time I appeared; I was there guest speaker for that morning.

Over the next few years, I needed Our Mission Corner perhaps more than the unchurched did. I was able to come with testimonies of myself and others, the mission field experiences of West Africa and the hunger, starvation and medical needs that we saw. I know the Holy Spirit sent me to that corner in Little-Five Points to be of help to others. They are not at their end; they heard testimonies and the Word of God preached and were moved to give their testimonies, songs, and prayer. I preached that through faith in the Lord, they can be delivered and saved into an eternal life with Christ Jesus.

TRANSLATION:

Those who trust in the Lord, and give their life unto Him, he promises to keep us and never to leave us alone. We get the sense He sends his angels to guard us and protect our going in and coming out. This covering isn't to suggest that nothing will happen to us in our life's daily journey, but we can feel secure that the Lord is with us in everything and we can depend on that.

Chapter Nineteen

HE LEADS ME

Roman 8:14 (NIV) Because those who are led by the Spirit of God are sons of God.

I'M HAVING A FEW issues with my health right now, I am going through recovery that the Lord promised. The Lord says,be patient, study your bible, pray for the church, and the un-churched while I am taking care of your issues. I was walking across my lawn one day, I saw a few scraps of paper, I leaned over and picked them up, then came this quiet still voice, Oscar "I am trying to heal you," I dropped what I had in my hand, stood their fulfilled with His presense and began to cry. We do unnecessary things that affect the Lord's blessing upon us.

I believe the Holy Spirit is telling me to be patient, let your body heal and stop trying to do physical work. Do the work I have given you and trust me with the rest of what is going on in, and around you. There were occasions the Lord call me a "knuckle head." In the Word this is disobedience, I have taken a step back and began to make better decision. I set down and began pending to the Lord the journals and the path He has set me own to tell others that He is the Giver of Gifts, that was promised from creation, we are call with a purpose to fulfill through Him.

Friday evening, I went to Tuskegee to do several things, including turn heat on in my house the temperatures have been very cold. I turned on the heat, and the water pipes had burst loose. I called for help from my friend, whom I have written about other times. He quickly called a friend, a plumber came over went up into the attic and made the repair. I knew in my spirit it was the Lord with His covering for me, because I had been praying that the Lord would protect the place until I arrived and turned the heat on.

Our friend buried her friend, and it has been rough for her. I had invited the Holy Spirit to let me know if there was something I should do while there. During the visit, the Holy Spirit led me to pray for her, and He would bless her with a ministry to visit others that are in need. When I wrote this, I felt the Lord presence, I said to myself, I inquired of the Lord for direction, I got this right, I was thankful.

Our class in High School, met and had our annual Christmas Dinner as a high school family. After dinner, we were sharing with each other about where have we been and what have we done in over forty-nine years since high school days. A few of us exchanged comments about some of our experiences and how the Lord is using us for his good. In general, I couldn't be sure where I stood being used by the Lord, I think most of us do our christian duty by going to church, Bible study and helping each other when and how ever we can. We are always kind, caring and always helpful, and with a kind spirit. Our Lord loves such children as this. At that time, I felt the presence of the Holy Spirit to pray for each other, Lord would bless our, every need for we are servant of the Lord. Even now when I pend this to the Lord, I felt his presence, almost to tears, we are to remember our Lord keeps his Word.

I love being led by the Holy Spirit, He takes us and places us where we ought be for his assignments, I felt the Lords presence when I wrote that statement.

My hope is those who read this, take it into your lives and believe that the Lord desires to Lead and Guide You into right places to do His assignments. He teaches me, if we take care of His assignment, He will take care of our health and other issues that will come our way.

TRANSLATION:

When a person becomes a Christian, he or she gains all the privileges and responsibilities of a child in God's family. One of these outstanding privileges is being led by the Spirit. He encourages us to ask God for what we want. We are joint heirs with Christ.

Chapter Twenty

IN HIS PRESENCE;
CONTINUALLY

Genesis 12:2 (NIV) I will make you into a great
nation and I will bless you; I will make your name
great, and you will be a blessing.

WE WERE HAVING DEVOTION this morning at a local
church, and from our devotional hymnal, this was read:
And of the angels he saith, Who maketh His Angels
Spirits, and His Ministers A Flame of Fire. Strangely,
almost a year to the date I received His presence and
now, I hear it again, and is moved by the scripture. I
comprehend that we have His pneumia (spirit to do
the work) He calls us to. The Holy Spirit lead and
guide us to teach us in all truth when we give our life
to Christ. I said yes, that I trust Him and would follow
His leading and guiding because I believe He does
everything for my good.

After devotion prayer, the minister began his scripture: Genesis 12:1-7 with this title, "The Impossible Dream," as he read the scripture, verse two, call out to me in the spirit. Genesis 12:2, I will make of you a great nation, and I will bless thee, and make thy name great; and thou shalt be a blessing: (3) And I will bless them that bless thee, and curse him that curseth thee: and in thee shall all families of the earth be blessed. I understand what it meant to Abraham and Sarah, today I don't know.

Part of verse two and three, I felt the spirit and it was felt strongly. I am thankful, I can pray and believe the Lord hears my prayers. It may be a time for now or the future. The overwhelming presence of the Lord today, I prayed for all those who were not well, who had extend absent from church and were present today and our pastors need our continual prayers and the blessings of good health and spiritual growth for the church.

The Holy Spirit started speaking early this morning, to check my health and make corrections. He gave me insight where I had the issue, and I understood. Late evening, a minister was preaching about going through issues and situations and said not to quit because we are going through tests. When I heard that, I felt His presence and this gave me a spiritual lift, and it encouraged me to stay the course, focused and stay on my assignment for the Lord and pray without ceasing.

TRANSLATION:

God promised to bless Abram and make him great, but God had one condition: Abram had to do what God wanted him to do, which was leave his home and friends and traveling to a new land where God promised to build a great nation from Abram's family. God may be trying to lead you to a place of greater service and usefulness for him. Don't let the comfort and security of your present position make you miss God's plan for you.

Chapter Twenty One

DAILY HE GROWS US

John 3:30 (NIV) He must become greater, I must become less.

THROUGH OUR PRAYERS, WE are seeking the Holy Spirit. We are looking for that closer walk with the Lord, we are asking Him to take us and make us over; so we can be used in the service of the Lord. The Holy Spirit hears our prayers and looks at our heart and see us growing towards Him, and begins a work in us. The Holy Spirit must bring us into a position of submission and change from the old man into the new man in Christ Jesus. He whispers to our heart, and we must decrease and allow Him to increase in us, and received the purpose He has planned for our lives.

We will learn to be led by the Holy Spirit, trusting the Lord and Him only. Today, the Lord brought increase into the life of our barber at the barbershop. She had just begun to give me a beard shape up, and I felt the prompting of the Holy Spirit to pray, and He will bless her to be a blessing to someone else. I began to feel His presence the barber is working to get my face shape up just right, I am getting fulfillment and I had to stop her.

My assignment, anointed her hands, and when this was done, the presence of The Holy Spirit was evident, and I was thankful to be part of her increase through the Holy Spirit. Candidly, after the prayer, I asked my barber what she had been praying for. She wanted the Lord to bless her hands in a way they can be used for His good, through her shop while working on clients in the barbershop. When working on the clients with her hands, she wanted the blessing to flow from the Holy Spirit through her to bless her clients in a way only the Lord would choose, only the Lord know of our needs.

Family, here is the response to obedience it is spoken all the time our Lord knows everything about us from our beginning, hear comes the training for increase, the barber had just finished my facial shape up and another customer walked in and asked how much to shape up his face because he didn't have enough money for a haircut. She gave him the amount for a facial shapeup, he approved. Sir would you mind if I treat you today, thank you he said, I paid for both our shape up. It feels good to bless others in the name of Jesus. I felt the presence to tell her to bless him with favor from the Lord, she gave a free haircut and completed his shape up.

My hope is that I heard the Lord correctly, and was obedient to the assignment. Writing this, is to ask others to listen for that still quiet voice from our Lord that it may strengthen others with the Lord, and be not afraid to expect your increase from the Lord.

TRANSLATION:

John, the Apostle of the Lord Jesus Christ's willingness to decrease in importance, shows unusual humility. Pastors and other Christian leaders can be tempted to focus more on the success of their ministries than on Christ Jesus, who can grow their ministries beyond measure. Let us be clear, our focus is always on the Lord, and clearly, He is to receive all the glory and the praise for the great works that are accomplished through His blessing.

Chapter Twenty Two

OUR GOD LOVES US

Psalm 37:5 (NIV) Commit yours way to the Lord; trust in him and he will do this.

I HEAR THE YOUNG owner speaking success into his future and the business with the tour company he is trying very hard to position himself to be prepared for additional work he believes the Lord will send his way. I am pending this because we won't ever really know how we'll turn out; so we are trusting the Lord and trying to follow His instruction. Our Lord does performs wonders, when we are trying to get it right, the Lord has a way of turning it around for our good, and His blessing is on those who trust in Him.

Our young owner is moving into the tour bus transportation and has aligned himself with other owners. His customer base is beginning to grow, but the market is starting to create uncertainty.

The down turn in the markets has created a tremendous loss of jobs with companies cutting costs, reducing payroll, and the cut back on tours. The young owner closed down his bus line, only a few of the long standing owners continued. They had a long standing customer base and they were able to lower rates to protect their customer base. He sold his fleet and purchased property in a excellent location. When the marketplace return, he will have the opportunity to return under the right circumstances.

Where is the Lord in all of this, The young owner had been up and down this business district and had not scene this sale sign before. On this day the for sale sign seem to jump out at him, he parked and called the number. I believe there was a presence that came to him to closed down and prepare for your return.

These testimonies that I am pending are to give us hope and grow our faith; God tells us, be of good courage, strengthening thine heart. When the Holy Spirit is speaking to us in this manner, we know He Loves Us, and we can trust and never doubt.

TRANSLATION:

David calls us to take delight in the Lord and to commit everything we have and our way to Him. To delight in someone means to experience great pleasure and joy in the presence of the Lord. We must get to know Him very well to enjoy His presence and have delight in Him, and we must have knowledge and understanding of God's great love for us.

Chapter Twenty Three

GOD'S GLORY AND MAN'S HONOR: MISSION CORNER

Psalm 8:1 (NIV) O Lord, our Lord, how majestic is your name in all the earth.

I HAD RAISED UP early and gone to the Local Church service. I often go and visit my brother at the nursing home afterward. This particular morning while sitting in service, I felt disappointed in myself, because I had missed visiting with my friends on the mission corner. I spoke to my conscious and said, I hadn't prepared a word from The Lord to speak to His children on our "Mission Corner" in Little-Five Points. I would come and greet those of us who are dealing with life's struggles, and sometimes we come as seekers, hopeful that someone would show up with a word that would speak to our needs, a word that would turn my life to Christ Jesus.

Dutiful, when I arrived I would see our elderly brother laboring on our streets for many years with words of wisdom, with insight through faith to help us to recovery who loves to have a song to lift everyone's spirit. Our young brother would set up tables with hot chocolate, tea, sodas and other snacks to tide the others over until service has ended and then feed them a fully prepared meal.

When our young brother comes before our friends on our mission corner, he seemed to always have the right scriptures and readings to those that are present need. This young brother invited me and encouraged me to come and share my testimonies and my experiences to the others. I know it will help others, because it helped me. Whenever I came, he received me and allowed me to participate, and I am so very thankful to him. He would call me and say, if you can make it to the corner this weekend bring us a word, we need it. Family this is a call for help, if each of us can share what the Lord has done in each of our lives we have answer the call.

While sitting in church, I felt a presence in my spirit to read Psalm 8:1, O Lord our Lord how excellent is thy name in all the earth who has set thy glory above the heavens. The Holy Spirit came upon me so strongly that I was brought to tears. I appeared with my christian brother that morning and brought the message the Lord had given me. I am certain many ministers pray and ask the Lord to provide a word to bring to the children. For me it showed up when least expected, there was a word, prayers of healing, and blessing that went out that morning. When I made the offer to those that wanted to follow Christ, a young woman raised her hand and gave her life to Christ Jesus. I am praying, when others read this, the Holy Spirit will come upon each of you and be fill with the awesome presence of the Holy Spirit and be blessed, that He will fill each of our particular needs.

The message is clear; Jesus came to us that we may share in the new covenant with Him, and sacrifices would end with Christ Jesus going to the cross at Calvary. A young woman and a young man gave there life to Christ at Our Mission Church at 11 am.

TRANSLATION:

God is to be glorified, for making known himself to us. Jesus became human, a little lower than heavenly beings, when the Father sent Him to the earth. When Jesus had ascended into heaven, the Father put everything under His feet. This is the church and removing all the evil from his children before Jesus Christ returns for His Bride.

Chapter Twenty Four

DON'T GIVE UP THE FIGHT

Exodus 14:14; The Lord Will Fight For You, You Need To Stand.

I MET A YOUNG student from out of town that had become the first student elected to the city council of that city. I asked how did he get my information, and he replied, "I was sharing my desire to help our city to grow. I am developing a model to renovate area's that need this model, with that explanation they volunteered my information how to contact me.

A few months later he called to review his business model and asked if I would be interested in investing in his housing upgrade and renovation plans. I explained to him during our session together that the Lord has called me into ministry and I am hanging up my tool belts to do His work. I was about to buy more land start building more houses, but the Lord got my attention;

it was time to serve Him and get busy fulfilling the purpose He has for my life.

At any rate, we reviewed the plans and, admittedly, they were very feasible. I addressed a few key concepts that must be in place to become a venture capitalist. A.) Have our Christ Jesus agreed with your plan? You can't raise a city from the dead that has been robbed and stripped for many years with out our Lord. If you have not done this, get it done. I gave him support to enlist help and advice to go for it, do the ground work. We had prayer, I asked the Lord to bless his effort and be merciful unto him and fulfill his planned to works.

I didn't hear from him for a long time, well over a year, I asked my friend how was this young man doing on his project. She informed me he had develop health issues and and was in recovery.

I was in the city for there first Mardi Gras, I saw him walking with his family was very happy to see he was doing well. Later, he introduced his wife to me and said he hoped to visit me in a couple of weeks. He called this afternoon, and we were talking, and with all the man in him, the Holy Spirit that has taken care of him, he recalled his promise from a few years ago to keep me informed on how he was doing, and he intended to keep that promise. I must confess in my spirit right now; I love him with the Love of Jesus for such a compelling move of sincerity and honesty of purpose.

During this encounter on the telephone, I felt the presence of the Holy Spirit, so I began to pray the blessing of the Holy Spirit upon his health and life, I felt a complete healing in him, and his blessing, he would achieve particular works because he is spiritually motivated to accomplish his work.

TRANSLATION:

The people were hostile and despairing, but Moses encouraged them to watch the wonderful ways God would rescue them. Moses had a positive attitude when it looked as if they were trapped, Moses called upon God to intervene. We may not be chased by an army, but we may still feel trapped. Instead of giving in to despair, we should adopt Moses's attitude to "stand firm" and see the deliverance the Lord will bring.

Chapter Twenty Five

HE BLESSES IN OUR STORMS

Job 1:22 (NIV) In all this, Job did not sin by charging God with wrong doing.

Job 1:6 (NIV) One day the angels came to present themselves before the Lord, and Satan "also came with them."

Job 6:30 (NIV) Is tasteless food eaten without salt, or is there flavor in the white of an egg.

IT IS WRITTEN ABOUT, preached, witnessed, and many testimonies will establish these facts that if you are going into are already in a storm, our first line of communication is go and tell Jesus all about what we believe your need is. Ask trusted friends and family to pray with you as the doctors determine the matter of your situation and the degrees of it. Know that the Holy Spirit is the first line of defense; Nothing touches the heart of the Lord more deeply than when we consult Him first and confess to the Lord, He is first, we can often receive the Lord's favor it is all in His will to do so.

I was asleep early Wednesday morning when I began to have a vision, seeing a cross in the beyond, and right after that, I heard a voice quite clearly say "Job, chapter one," and I said to myself, I should write this down, but I will remember. A few seconds later, I heard chapter 6 and I repeated this to myself, "I need to read chapter one and chapter six." I was curious because I had been told by a prophetess that the Holy Spirit had laid this on her spirit to give this to me. In November of 2010, there was this special trip made that she would witness to me the assignment to read Job and know that it would demand daily prayer, understanding the covering in the blood of Jesus with His hedge of protection. This drew sharp concerns because Job engaged tremendous storms and sharp criticism from his thought-to-be friends. In Job 1:1-22, Satan obtains permission to tempt Job, this subtitle suggests Job is in a serious storm; he is an upright man before God and his fellow man in early times respected him. In chapter six, Job justifies his complaints to Eliphaz, with little or no benefit. Let's be mindful; trusting friends isn't like trusting the Lord and the Lord only, who knows all things about you and your needs. The Lord is your first authority and the last word for your benefit.

I pray that we remember, no matter how bad it gets, or what it looks like, to trust the Holy Spirit at all times in all things. Friendship is a great comfort when we are in trials and tribulations, but even so, beware of advice from them that sounds like affirmation; unless you are certain this is of God, stay in prayer and seek the Lord. In a storm we can't determine all the Lord is saying to us, we need our trusted pastor, prayer family that we know. In this approach we often get it right.

TRANSLATION:

VS. 22. Job has lost all when evil touches his life, but he reacted rightly toward God by acknowledging God's has sovereign authority over all things that he gives us.

VS. 6. The devil can't be in only one place at a time, the fallen angels do his evil work, the devil is limited, he must get approval from the Lord before he can tempt us, and he can't see into our mind; if he could have, he would have known Job's mind and wouldn't have tempted Job.

VS. 30. Job's defense of himself was based on the kind of life he had lived. He had integrity, not that he was sinless, but did live with high moral standards and treated others as he wanted to be treated, and from this, others had great respect for him. Job knew he had a right relationship with the Lord his Savior, and tried to obey the Lord to the best of his ability.

Chapter Twenty Six

HER MIRACLE

Galatians 3:5 (NIV) Does God give you His Spirit and work miracles among you because you observe the law, or because you believe what you heard?

LATE THIS EVENING I went over to the Care Facility, and it was later than I like to go over. When I don't go over often, I feel like the families have been neglected by me. I arrived in the evening I visited my friend, who is doing well. She reads and enjoy conversation so I am not in a hurry. My elderly friend went through a rough time a few months ago. She lost her appetite, and became so weak she needed assistance with everything.

One particular day, I was praying for her and blessing the family that supports her, and while praying, these words came out of my mouth to bless her food with the taste of "a sweet, sweet honey comb," like the words David spoke about the precepts of the Lord to him was sweeter than a sweet honeycomb. The Holy Spirit brought forth a "miracle" for the great-grand mother, and after a few weeks, she was restored and eating well. Our God is an awesome God, aside from Him we can do nothing.

Today, months later, I am still visiting her and others as I complete my work doing prayer and scriptures. During my visits, I rarely ask visitors if they have a prayer request. Today, I asked a little girl, who must have been eight or ten years old. She shook her head no, but her grandmother interceded and said, "Why don't you ask him to pray for your arm? You have been asking everyone else. This is the minister who prayed for Great Grandmother, show him your arm, the little girl stretched out her arms and you could easily see the right arm was short and the left arm was normal.

Just as I started to contemplate, saying to the Lord this little girl is expecting results, at that moment I felt the fulfilling presence of the Holy Spirit, I was thankful. The Lord will lead me in right prayer, I began to exalt His name in prayer for the little girl. I took her right arm in my hand and had her sit straight, and I heard a little noise as I was holding her arm out as I prayed. When I had finished, I said in a low voice, I heard something, and great grandmother said out loud that she heard something also. I felt better after that explanation, I had the little girl place her arms and fingers evenly together and stretched them out before us, they looked even. Great Grandmother looked at me with a grateful heart, the Lord had fixed great grand-baby arm, the children want make fun anymore. I was somewhat surprised.

My little friend seemed fine with what had transpired. My prayers was full of praise and glory to the Lord. I thanked and praised Him for Her Miracle that He had given this little girl. I prayed and blessed her with an anointing on her life, I feel this in my spirit, she has a special calling from on High "for I have chosen you." I thank the Lord for using me to bless the child and bring praise and glory to His name.

TRANSLATION:

The Holy Spirit gives Christians great power to live for God. Often the Holy Spirit's greatest work is teaching us to persist, to keep on doing what is right even when it no longer seems interesting or exciting. Know that you are working for the Lord.

Chapter Twenty Seven

BE IN HIS WILL

Luke 6:19 (NIV) And the people all tried to touch Him because power was coming from Him and healing them all.

I HAVE BEEN VISITING my natural-pathic doctor, I feel we have an excellent relationship. I think all his patients will say the same, because he is so very complete in working with each of us, especially when we plug in the fact that he prays for his clients for an understanding of their needs.

On this last Saturday, there was a powerful working of the Holy Spirit through two lady assistants that are powerful spiritual ladies that support the doctor and are in training. Before they could assist him to work on me, I had to bless them through the Holy Spirit, and the doctor began with prayer welcoming the Holy Spirit and angels to assist us. Each of us have a special purpose in working with healing and the most important point I want to make is the guidance that is sought before, the majority of the time, the Holy Spirit has spoken an approach to be used on me. We have access to our angels, I believe this, I assign them task to help me as well as others that the Lord lead me to pray for and assist us in our recovery. I been in hospital, nursing and rehabilitation centers I take the Lord at His Word. Psalms 107:20; Jesus bore my sickness and carried my pain. Therefore I give no place to sickness or pain. For God sent His Word and healed me.

When I got to the doctor's office and listed the areas for him to work on, he had the equipment already setup to work on my issues. The Spirit had already given understanding through prayer what was to be done.

The assistants and the natural-pathic doctor provided powerful working on my issues, I like getting accupuncture needles they help move energy through the body. Family I am in my mid seventies we get stagnant energy throughout our bodies, we feel sluggish, our get up and go seemingly have left us. I get help through none-evasive therapy, our prayers were for a complete healing and we are thankful that we were in agreement through the Holy Spirit to bless his servant. When the session was going on, I was in meditation I was giving thanks to the Lord for His blessing and will continually have praising for His wonderful works.

My feeling is that all we have prayed for, I have received. I am thanking the Lord for His many blessings of good health and strength to continue to work for His Kingdom. I know that the Lord is good to me, and I love His spirit of inspiration that continues to encourage me to continue to work.

With the love of the Lord, I encourage each of us to stay encouraged.

TRANSLATION:

When the news of Jesus healing power spread, crowds gathered just to touch Him. Jesus had become a symbol of good fortune, for healing and other needs. There should have been efforts to find forgiveness and draw closer to Him, and discover the love in Him that He is willing to share. They perhaps didn't know He could pardon their sins; we should seek him sincerely and be led by the Holy Spirit. In this relationship, we will discover through seeking Him; first, all the other things we are standing in need of, the Lord can fulfill.

We should readily impart to others what God has trusted to us, rejoicing to make others joyful, especially taking pleasure in communing with those who believe.

ABOUT THE AUTHOR

OSCAR I. DIXON, SR.

I was born in Roba, Alabama, August 29, 1942 to Ethel and Rev. Frank D. Dixon, he was a pastor in the Alabama A. M. E. Zion Church Conference. I gave my life to Christ at a very early age, about ten or eleven years old, and were baptized and joined The County Line A. M. E. Zion Church, under the pastorate of Reverend Robert Day. Through prayer and fasting, I learned, I was called into the ministry at the tender age of fourteen by our Lord, Jesus Christ. As I grew up, I had many encounters from my youth to adulthood, my parents, explained these events, and finally they said we were peculiar children. I am married, to Mrs. Gloria Allen Dixon, for over 53 years with two children, Oscar Lee and Melinda Rae Dixon Chapman. We are grandparents to Oscar Najee and

Natosha Dixon Porter, who gives us two great grands, Imani and Zechariah.

Oscar Dixon, Sr. When the Lord called me this time, he got my attention, I had retired from my job, and was in my late fifties. I had built houses and was renovating properties. Doing this time, I became very sick and, I didn't feel so deserving, but the Lord turned my fears into joy. My church family new of my struggles with my health and they prayed without ceasing. I remember my pastor saying to me, brother Oscar, we are praying for you. Why working on my property, the Lord call my name, He asked me "Will You Serve Me," I said yes and I have not looked back, but sought every opportunity to prepare myself to be able to serve. I took my theology studies from Beacon University, Columbus, Georgia, I achieved my Associate Degree, and Bachelors Degree of Theology. From the Christian Life Studies of Theology, I achieved my Master's Degree of Theology in 2013. I have three years in the The African Methodist Episcopal Zion Church studies. In 2005, I was invited to come on a mission trip into downtown Atlanta, I am still here working in 2017. I volunteered to work in two health and rehabilitation facility, I began in 2007 and 2008. There is a take away in this spiritual focus, remember when you pray, believe what you have prayed for, and receive it has though it has already manifested itself, because The Lord answers prayers.

www.ingramcontent.com/pod-product-compliance
Lightning Source LLC
Chambersburg PA
CBHW072201090426
42740CB00012B/2340